CHARLIE BROWN'S 'CYCLOPEDIA

Super Questions and Answers and Amazing Facts

Featuring
Sound, Light and Air

Volume 14

Based on the Charles M. Schulz Characters

Funk & Wagnalls, Inc.

Photograph and Illustration Credits: Association of American Railroads, 671; Bell Laboratories, 644; The Bettman Archive, Inc., 637; The Cousteau Society, 659; © Four By Five, 671; © Fundamental Photographs, 633, 645, 658; Honeywell, Inc., 650; Richard Megna/Fundamental Photographs © 1980, 632; Richard Megna/Fundamental Photographs © 1981, 647; The Metropolitan Museum of Art, Gift of Mrs. Henry McSweeney, 1959, 627; The Metropolitan Museum of Art, Gift of Mrs. John H. Lufbery and Shirley Sammis Foulds, 1978, 628; The Metropolitan Museum of Art, The Crosby Brown Collection of Musical Instruments, 1889, 630; The Metropolitan Museum of Art, The Crosby Brown Collection of Musical Instruments, 1889, and Gift of the University of Pennsylvania, 1953, 631; Museum of Modern Art/Film Stills Archive, 641; National Oceanic & Atmospheric Administration, 661; Courtesy, National Center for Atmospheric Research, ix; Smithsonian Institution Photo No. 46838, 663.

A large part of this volume was previously published in *Charlie Brown's Fifth Super Book of Questions and Answers.*

Introduction

Welcome to volume 14 of *Charlie Brown's 'Cyclopedia*! Have you ever wondered how a piano works, or what makes movies move, or what "scuba" means? Charlie Brown and the rest of the *Peanuts* gang are here to help you find the answers to these questions and many more about sound, light, and air. Have fun!

Sound, Light, and Air

What is sound?

Sound is what you hear when something vibrates—moves back and forth quickly. If you stretch a rubber band and twang it, you can see the vibrations that cause the sound. You can also see them when you pluck a guitar string.

Anything that vibrates makes the air around it vibrate. The vibrating air makes the insides of your ears vibrate. That's how you hear. Usually you can't see any vibrations when you hear a sound. But the vibrations are still there. Sound vibrations travel through most other materials, as well as through air.

Why are some sounds low and others high?

The sound coming from a vibrating object will be high or low depending on how many vibrations it makes each second. A low sound, like that made by a foghorn, has slow vibrations. A high sound, like that made by a whistle, has fast vibrations. The lowest sounds that most people can hear have about 20 vibrations per (each) second. The highest sounds people can hear have about 20,000 vibrations per second. Some animals, such as bats and dolphins, can hear very high sounds—more than 100,000 vibrations per second. The scientific word for the number of vibrations per second is "hertz." It is abbreviated Hz. A scientist would say people can hear sounds between 20 and 20,000 hertz.

How do musical instruments make sounds?

All musical instruments make air vibrate. But they don't all do it in the same way. Some have strings that vibrate. Others have small pieces of wood called reeds that vibrate. With some instruments, the vibrations come from the player's lips. Drums, cymbals, and xylophones vibrate when somebody strikes them.

Most instruments are made so that the player can control how high or low the sound will be.

LOW SOUNDS...
HIGH SOUNDS...
GOOD GRIEF, IT'S
SOUND POLLUTION!

How does a piano work?

Attached to every piano key is a hammer. This is a piece of wood covered with a felt pad. When you press a key, the hammer hits a small group of metal strings. Most pianos have 230 strings.

The pitch (highness or lowness of the sound) of each string depends on how long and thick the string is and how tightly it is stretched. Short, thin strings have a higher pitch than long, thick strings. The tighter you stretch a string, the higher its pitch will be. Some of the strings are wrapped with wire to make them vibrate more slowly.

In 1935, a giant-sized piano was built. Its longest string was 9 feet 11 inches (about 3 meters). That's probably more than twice your height!

627

How does a guitar make music?

A guitar has strings that make sounds when you pluck them with your fingers. The strings are stretched across a pear-shaped box. Without this box, the strings would make a very faint sound. With the box, the sound is amplified (AMP-luh-fied), made louder.

The pitch of a guitar note depends on two things: the thickness and the tightness of the strings. In that way a guitar is like a piano. But on a guitar, you can change the pitch by pressing a string with your finger. When you do this, you are cutting short the part of the string that vibrates. So, in a way, you are making the string shorter. Banjos, mandolins, and ukuleles work in much the same way.

Violin

Does a violin work the same way as a guitar?

Not quite. A violin has strings like a guitar. When you play a violin, you control the pitch by pressing on the strings—as you do with a guitar. But instead of plucking the strings to make them vibrate, you rub a bow across the strings. The bow is a wooden stick with horsehairs stretched between the ends. Sound vibrations are made when the hairs rub on the violin strings.

 Imagine playing a violin under water! Mark Gottlieb did it as a stunt in 1975.

What is a wind instrument?

A wind instrument is any instrument that makes a sound when someone blows into it. A horn, a kazoo, and a saxophone are all wind instruments.

A wind instrument has a body made of a long or short tube. When you blow into the instrument, air vibrates inside the tube. The longer the tube, the lower the pitch. Most wind instruments have push buttons on, or holes in, the tube. That's where you put your fingers when you play the instrument. When you press a button or uncover a hole, the pitch is changed. The pitch changes because the amount of space left for the air to vibrate in changes.

There are two main kinds of wind instruments. They are called brass instruments and woodwind instruments.

629

What are brass instruments like?

Bugles, trumpets, cornets, trombones, tubas, French horns, and sousaphones are brass instruments. They all have very long tubes that are folded back and forth or curled around and around. This makes the instrument easier to carry than if the long tube were straight. As you might guess, brass instruments are made of brass.

If you want to play a brass instrument, you must press your lips together and make a buzzing sound like "p-f-f-f-t" when you blow into the tube. When you go "p-f-f-f-t," your lips vibrate. This makes the air in the instrument vibrate.

Hunting horn

L.V. BEETHOVEN

TROMBONE

FRENCH HORN

TUBA

THIS IS A GREAT WAY TO MEET SOME REALLY NEAT CHICKS.

630

How are woodwind instruments played?

Woodwind players don't go "p-f-f-f-t." Instead, they blow air across one or two thin pieces of wood called reeds. Or else they blow across a hole at one end of the instrument. Clarinets, oboes, bassoons, and saxophones are played by blowing across reeds. Blowing makes the reeds vibrate. Flutes and piccolos are played by blowing across a hole. Blowing across the hole makes the air inside the instrument vibrate.

Once all woodwinds were made of wood. Today, some are made of plastic or metal.

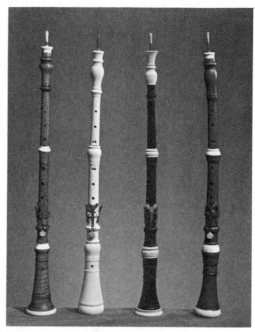

Oboes

631

How does a stethoscope help a doctor listen to your heart?

A stethoscope lets the doctor listen with both ears. Before stethoscopes were invented, doctors had to listen to hearts by pressing one ear against the patient's chest. Now they can use both ears and hear better.

A stethoscope has two listening pieces to help the doctor hear different kinds of sounds. The small disc piece is good for listening to very low-pitched sounds. The large disc piece is good for listening to higher sounds. The sounds travel from the listening pieces through rubber tubes to the doctor's ears. The next time you go for a checkup, ask the doctor to let you listen to your heart with the stethoscope.

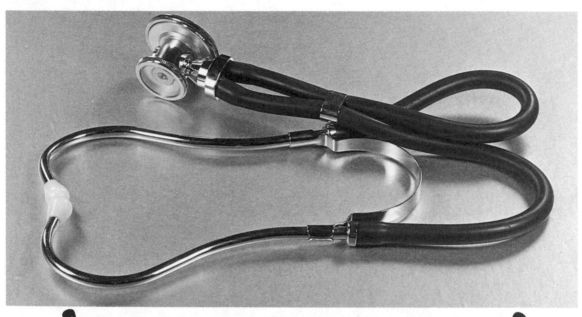

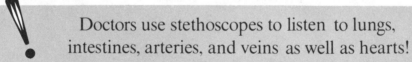

Doctors use stethoscopes to listen to lungs, intestines, arteries, and veins as well as hearts!

What is a prism?

A prism is a bar of glass with flat sides. A good prism has no bubbles or ripples in it. When a beam of sunlight passes through a prism, the light spreads out into separate beams of color. The colors are the same as you would see in a rainbow—red, orange, yellow, green, blue, and violet. In fact, a rainbow in the sky is caused by drops of water in the air that act like prisms. A drop of water can change sunlight into colored beams of light, just like a prism.

How does a prism cause a rainbow?

A beam of sunlight is really a mixture of light waves of many colors. Light travels in the form of waves. Each color of light has its own kind of wave. Red light waves are long. Violet light waves are short. The other colors are in between.

When light waves enter a prism, they bend. And they bend again when they come out of the other side of the prism. The various colors bend by different amounts. Because of this, the colors spread out as they pass through the prism. The colors line up side by side instead of being mixed together. And you can see the separate colors of the rainbow.

Light shining through prism

633

Why does a mirror show a picture of what's in front of it?

A mirror shows a picture, called a reflected image, because the mirror has a thick shiny silver-colored coating behind the glass. The silver-colored coating does two things:

1. It keeps light waves from passing through the mirror. Since they can't go through, they bounce back toward your eyes.

2. It makes the mirror *very* shiny.

When light waves bounce off a dull, unshiny surface, they scatter and go every which way. But when the waves bounce off something shiny, they don't scatter.

When you stand in front of a mirror, light waves move from you to the shiny mirror. The light waves then bounce right back off the mirror in exactly the same way they hit the mirror. And you see yourself!

634

How does a magnifying glass make things look big?

A magnifying glass plays a trick on your eyes. It does this by changing the direction of light waves coming from the object you are looking at. The curved surfaces of the glass bend the waves, and it appears to your eyes that the waves are coming from a big object.

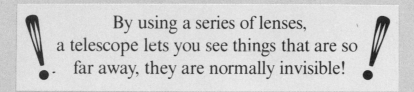

By using a series of lenses, a telescope lets you see things that are so far away, they are normally invisible!

By using two or three magnifying lenses, a microscope lets you see things that are so small, they are normally invisible!

How do eyeglasses and contact lenses help some people see better?

When you look at something, you see it because waves of light are coming from it. When some of these enter your eye, they form a picture of what you are looking at. This picture appears on the back surface of the inside eye.

When light waves enter the eye, they pass through the curved front end called the cornea. Then they pass through a part called the lens. The combination of cornea and lens is supposed to focus, or aim, the light waves so that the picture on the back of the eye will be clear and sharp. Some people's eyes cannot do this very well. So they have blurry vision. Other people have eyeballs that are either too long or too short from front to back. If an eyeball is too long or too short, it is hard for it to form a good picture on the back surface of the eye.

Eyeglasses and contact lenses are extra glass or plastic lenses put in front of the eyes' own lenses. The glasses or contacts help eyes with blurry vision by doing part of the work of aiming or bending the light waves. Then the waves can come together at the right place at the back of the eye.

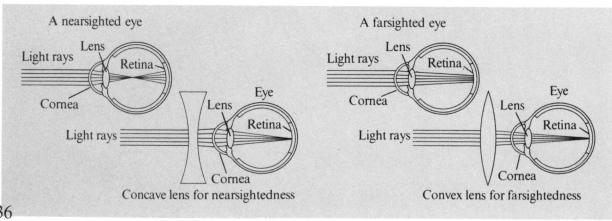

How are bifocals different from other eyeglasses?

Regular eyeglasses have one simple lens for each eye. The lens helps a person see either nearby things better or faraway things better. Bifocals have one lens with two parts for each eye. One part helps someone see nearby things better. Another part helps the person see faraway things better.

Benjamin Franklin invented bifocals in 1785. Before that time, people who needed glasses to see clearly both far and near things had to carry around two pairs. But with bifocals such people need only one pair.

Benjamin Franklin

637

How does a camera make photographs?

A camera works very much like an eye. Light waves enter the front of a camera through a set of lenses. The lenses focus the light to form a picture on the inside back wall of the camera. To make photographs, you need a roll of film in your camera. Photographic film is a strip of plastic coated with special chemicals. These chemicals change when light hits them. The camera is made to hold part of the roll of film against the back wall of the camera. When you press the button to take a picture, light comes into the camera for a very short time—usually less than a second. The light waves shine on the film. They change the chemicals so that a picture will appear when the film is developed.

638

How is film developed?

When you take your film to be developed, the person you give it to sends it to a laboratory. There the film is taken into a darkroom and unrolled. The developing has to be done in the dark because light would ruin your pictures. The film is dunked into a tank of liquid chemicals. These chemicals change the color of the chemicals on your film in such a way that pictures are formed. These pictures are called negatives. Negatives show the objects in the picture with their right shapes but the wrong colors.

Next, each negative is placed over a piece of photographic paper. Photographic paper is coated with chemicals on one side. This is the paper from which your finished photographs will be made. When the negative is over the paper, a light is turned on for a few seconds. The light shines through the negative and casts a picture on the photographic paper. The picture is like a shadow of the negative. The paper remains blank, but the light shining on it causes invisible changes in the chemicals.

Next, the paper is placed in a pan of liquid chemicals. These liquids change the chemicals on the paper. Slowly, as the chemicals change, the finished photograph appears.

639

How can x-rays take a picture of a person's insides?

X-rays are like light waves, but they are much shorter. Scientists have built machines that shoot beams of x-rays just as flashlights shoot beams of visible light. Machines that shoot beams of x-rays are called x-ray machines. When light waves hit a person, they bounce off. But when x-rays hit a person, they go right through—just like light through a piece of glass. In this way, light waves and x-rays behave differently. But when light waves or x-rays hit a piece of photographic film, they behave the same. Both kinds of waves change the chemicals on the film. To make an x-ray picture of a person's insides, the x-ray machine shoots rays through the person onto a piece of photographic film. When the film is developed, it shows a shadowy picture of all the bones and other things inside the body.

The man who discovered x-rays, Wilhelm Roentgen (RENT-gun), didn't understand what they were. That's why he called the rays *x*!

I WONDER IF THAT MEANT THEY WERE X-RATED! HEE HEE HEE...

Series of photographs taken of running horse

What makes movies move?

If you look at a piece of movie film, you can see that it is just a long strip of photographs on a plastic strip. Each photograph is a tiny bit different from those on each side of it. If the film is of someone running or jumping or diving, you can see that the arms and legs are in different positions in different pictures. When you show the film in a projector, the projector flashes the pictures on a screen one at a time. The pictures flash on the screen very fast. You see 16 or more separate photos in just one second. When the pictures flash by that fast, your brain can't tell that your eyes are looking at many separate photos. You think you are looking at only one picture—a picture that moves.

How are cartoon movies made?

Cartoon characters are just drawings, and they can't move. But it is possible to play a trick on people's eyes so that it looks as if the characters are moving. To do this, artists draw thousands of pictures on separate clear plastic sheets called cels. Each picture shows a character in a slightly different position.

For each scene, the artists paint a background. One or more cels are put on top of the background. The combination is photographed by a special movie camera. (It takes only one picture each time a button is pressed. The usual movie camera keeps taking one picture after another.) Then the cels just photographed are taken off the background. Cels that look just a bit different from the first are placed over the same background. A second picture is photographed. In fact, one picture is taken for each tiny bit of movement a character is supposed to be making. When the film is shown through a movie projector, the characters appear to move. If you look at a strip of cartoon film, you can see how the characters change slightly from one picture to the next.

Who invented movies?

No one knows for sure. In the 1880s and 1890s many people were working on ways to make and project moving pictures. In 1891 Thomas Edison, the man who invented the electric light, built the first kinetoscope (kin-ET-uh-scope). This was a cabinet with a peephole. Inside were reels of film that turned. One person at a time looked into the peephole to see the movie. Some people believe that Edison's helper, William Dickson, invented the kinetoscope not Edison.

What is a laser?

A laser is a machine that shoots a thin, very high-powered beam of light. This beam is called a laser beam. Some laser beams are so powerful that they can burn holes in metal.

Laser being used in research

How does a laser work?

A laser beam starts out as a flash of ordinary light from a bright lamp. Light is a kind of energy, and it travels in waves or ripples. Ordinary light waves are jumbled. They spread out and go in all directions. A laser unjumbles the waves. It packs them side by side so that they all ripple up and down together. When the light waves are packed together like this, they will travel in a very straight line and not spread out. These light waves make up a laser beam.

How do people use lasers?

Many uses have been found for lasers. Laser beams are much hotter than other light beams. Their heat can be used to weld or cut tiny things. Sometimes surgeons use a laser instead of a knife to perform delicate operations on the insides of people's eyes.

Laser beams can travel farther than other light beams. In one test, a laser was used to shoot down an aircraft two miles away. Scientists can measure exactly how far it is from the earth to the moon by bouncing a laser beam off the moon.

644

How does a thermometer tell the temperature?

The most common type of thermometer is a hollow glass tube that holds a liquid. Usually the liquid is mercury or colored alcohol. When the temperature goes up, the liquid expands, or gets bigger. It takes up more space inside the tube. So the liquid rises in the tube. When the temperature falls, the liquid contracts, or gets smaller. It fills less space. So the liquid moves down the tube.

Along the glass tube are numbers. These numbers mark off small sections called degrees. The symbol for degree is a tiny circle next to the number, like this: 32°.

Sometimes you will see 50° F. or 10° C. The F. stands for Fahrenheit (FAIR-un-hite). The C. stands for Celsius (SELL-see-us). These are the most common kinds of thermometer measurements. Each kind uses a different range of numbers. But they both measure the same thing—how hot or cold it is where the thermometer is.

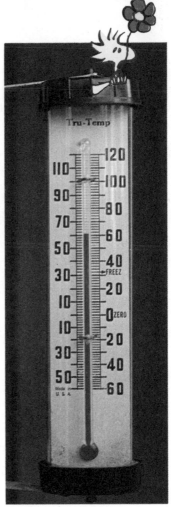

Outdoor thermometer

OOOOoo!! THAT'S COLD!

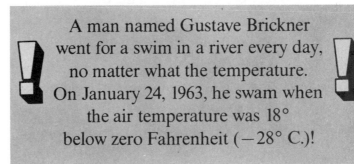

A man named Gustave Brickner went for a swim in a river every day, no matter what the temperature. On January 24, 1963, he swam when the air temperature was 18° below zero Fahrenheit (−28° C.)!

Do all thermometers look alike?

No. For example, oven and refrigerator thermometers are called bimetallic (by-muh-TAL-ick) thermometers. "Bimetallic" means two metals. This kind of thermometer has a spring made of two metals.

Metals expand when heated and contract when cooled. A bimetallic thermometer uses two different kinds of metal. One expands and contracts more than the other. Thin strips of the two metals are joined side by side. Then they are rolled up to make the spring. The spring is connected to a pointer. When the temperature rises, one of the metal strips winds up tighter than the other. This causes the pointer to move in one direction and not the other. The pointer swings to a higher number. When the temperature falls, the pointer moves in the other direction. It points to a lower number.

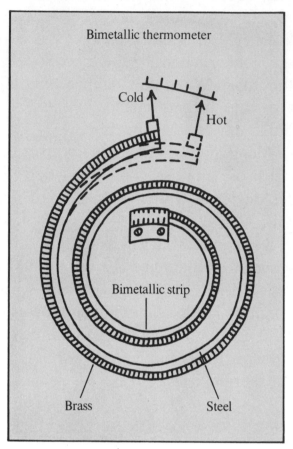

Bimetallic thermometer

How does a furnace make a whole house warm?

When coal, gas, or oil is burned inside a furnace, heat is produced. The heat can be moved from the furnace to other places in a house in at least three different ways.

1. The furnace heats air. A blower pushes warm air from the furnace through tunnels called ducts. The ducts lead to openings in all parts of the house.

2. The furnace heats water in a boiler. When the water boils, it turns to steam. The pressure of the steam makes it go through pipes to radiators in each room.

3. The furnace heats water in a boiler. A pump then sends the hot water through pipes to radiators. When the radiators become hot, they warm the air in the rooms.

How does a radiator warm a room?

A hot radiator warms the air next to it. The warmer the air gets, the lighter it becomes. Light air rises. So the warm, light air rises toward the ceiling. That should leave airless space near the floor by the radiator. But the gap is instantly filled by cool air that moves in from other parts of the room. This cool air becomes warm next to the radiator. And then *it* rises. The rising of the warm air and the movement of cool air toward the radiator is called convection (kun-VECK-shun). Convection is like a tiny wind that spreads the heat of the radiator all through the air in the room.

Red pieces of paper in boiling water show convection pattern

647

What is solar heating?

Solar heating uses wave energy that comes to us from the sun. In recent years, oil and gas have become scarce and expensive. People have realized that the burning of coal pollutes the air. So scientists and inventors have been searching for new ways to heat houses. One way is to capture heat from sunshine. Even in winter, there is a lot of heat coming to us in the form of waves from the sun. The problem is how to catch this heat energy and bring it indoors before it gets away.

How can people catch the sun's heat?

The most common solar heat collector is a low, flat box. It has a glass or plastic window on top. Most of the sun's light waves can pass easily through the glass or plastic. The inside of the box is painted black. This is because dark colors absorb, or soak up, the incoming light waves. Light colors reflect the waves, or make them bounce away.

The collector box is placed outdoors, usually on a roof facing the sun. The box is sealed very tightly. So none of the heat that enters through the window can get away. When the sun is shining, the box becomes hot inside. This is true even in winter.

The next step is to bring the heat from the box into the house. This is done with water pipes and a pump. Cool water is pumped from the house to pipes inside the collector box. The heat in the collector warms the water in the pipes. A pipe takes the warm water back into the house. There it can be pumped through a radiator, or used for washing or bathing. Sometimes it goes into a storage tank. If the water stayed too long in the tank, it would get cold. So it is pumped back up to the collector box to get heated again.

What makes a furnace turn on and off by itself?

Furnaces in houses and other buildings are controlled by thermostats (THUR-muh-stats). A thermostat turns the furnace on when the building is cool and off when the building is warm. A thermostat has a bimetallic spring, just like the thermometer you use in an oven or refrigerator. When the room temperature rises, the spring stretches in one direction. It turns off an electric switch. When the temperature falls, the spring stretches in the other direction. It turns the switch back on. You can set a thermostat to keep a house at any fairly steady temperature that you choose.

What other things use thermostats?

Many things that work by heating or cooling use thermostats. Refrigerators, air conditioners, ovens, electric frying pans, and electric blankets all have thermostats. If you set an air conditioner's thermostat at 75° F. (24° C.), it will keep the temperature of the room fairly steady. As soon as the air gets cooler, the air conditioner shuts off. As soon as the air gets warmer, the air conditioner turns on again.

What makes a refrigerator cold inside?

A refrigerator is a machine for taking heat out of a closed box. Cold is what is left in the box after the heat is taken out. The working of a refrigerator is based on one special fact: a liquid absorbs, or soaks up, heat when it evaporates (ih-VAP-uh-rates). When a liquid evaporates, it changes into a gas.

A refrigerator has a metal tube filled with a liquid that evaporates very fast. Part of the tube is inside the food box. Part of the tube is outside— underneath the refrigerator or on the back. If the inside of the food box gets warm, a thermostat turns on the refrigerator's motor. This makes the liquid flow through the tube. When the liquid enters the part of the tube that is *in* the food box, the liquid evaporates. It soaks up heat. Because the liquid has evaporated, the tube leading out of the food box is filled with gas. The tube leads to a compressor (come-PRESS-ur). A compressor squeezes the gas and changes it back into a liquid. When the gas is changed into a liquid, it gives off heat. So the compressor becomes hot. The heat goes into the air of the kitchen as the liquid moves through the part of the tube outside the refrigerator. The liquid again enters the food box. There it evaporates and soaks up more heat

FREON GAS

LIQUID FREON

MOTOR

COMPRESSOR

652

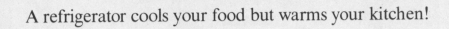
How does an air conditioner make a room cool?

An air conditioner works exactly the same as a refrigerator. But instead of taking heat out of a food box and putting it into the kitchen, it takes heat out of a room and puts it outdoors.

Part of a room-sized air conditioner is inside a window. This part has a cold tube filled with evaporating liquid. Part of the air conditioner is outside the window. This part has a compressor and a tube that gives off heat. An air conditioner also has a fan that blows air past the cold tube and out into the room. In this way all the air in the room gets a chance to be cooled by being blown past the cold tube.

653

How does a Thermos bottle keep milk cold?

"Thermos" is a brand name for a vacuum (VACK-yoom) bottle. A vacuum bottle works by insulating (IN-suh-late-ing) whatever you store in it. This means that when you store something cold, like milk, the bottle lets in very little heat. When you store something hot, like cocoa, the bottle lets very little heat get out.

A vacuum bottle is built like a bottle within a bottle. There is a narrow space between the two bottles. Almost all the air has been pumped out of this space. An empty space with no air or almost no air in it is called a vacuum. The vacuum keeps air from touching the inside bottle. It is important to keep the amount of air small because air can carry heat to cold things and take heat away from hot things.

Some heat can get through a vacuum. But much of this heat is blocked by the bottle's shiny, silvery coating. Heat, which travels in waves, bounces off shiny, silvery things. The bottle, being made of glass, also helps to insulate what is in it. Heat does not travel easily through glass.

654

How does a percolator make coffee?

A percolator is a machine for automatically pouring hot water on ground-up coffee beans. When hot water washes over the ground coffee, part of the beans dissolve in the water. That becomes the liquid coffee that people drink.

When the water in the bottom of a percolator starts to boil, it gives off bubbles of steam. Steam bubbles are lighter than water, and so they float up from the bottom. Most of them go up through the hollow tube that holds up the coffee basket. The bubbles rush up the narrow stem. Any water that gets in the way is pushed up the stem, too. That water squirts out the top of the stem. Then it drips down through the coffee basket. As it passes over the ground coffee, it becomes coffee-flavored.

655

How does a washing machine get clothes clean?

All a washer really does is make dirty clothes flop around in soapy water for a few minutes. It is the soap that gets the clothes clean. The most important part of a top-loader is called the agitator (AJ-ih-tay-tur). The agitator sticks up in the middle of the tub. It turns one way and then the other, back and forth. The paddles on the agitator poke and stir the clothes so that they move around in the water. After several minutes, the dirty water is pumped out. Clean water comes in to rinse the soap out of the clothes. Then the rinse water is pumped out, and the clothes are ready for drying.

How does a drier take the water out of wet laundry?

Wet clothes become dry because the water that is in them evaporates. When water evaporates, it changes to water vapor, a kind of gas, and goes off into the air. A clothes drier is a machine that makes evaporation take place quickly. It does this by blowing air on the clothes while they are tumbling around. Usually the air is warmed by a gas flame or an electric heater. This makes the water in the clothes evaporate quickly. Heat makes the tiny particles of water jump off into the air. Also, hot air can hold more water vapor than cold air can.

What makes a fire hose squirt far?

Two things—a pump and a nozzle. The pump is inside the fire truck that carries the hose. The pump pushes the water through the hose. The water goes through the hose in a wide, heavy, slow stream. But then the water comes to the metal nozzle at the end of the hose. The nozzle is much narrower than the hose. The nozzle squeezes the moving water into a thin, fast stream. Such a stream can go farther than a thick, slow stream. If you have a garden hose, try using it with a nozzle and without a nozzle. You will see that the nozzle makes the water squirt farther.

How does a water pistol shoot?

The trigger of a water pistol is connected to a small pump. When you pull the trigger, the pump makes some water move through a tube. Then the water squirts out through a nozzle in the front of the pistol. When you let go of the trigger, a spring pushes the trigger out and also refills the pump. You are then ready for the next shot.

How does a scuba-diving tank work?

The scuba tank holds compressed air. "Compressed" means that a lot is squeezed into a small space. If you let all the air out of a scuba tank, it could fill a whole room. A little bit of air at a time goes from the tank through a hose to a diver's mouth.

The most important parts of a scuba outfit are the valves. They control the amount of gas or liquid that goes through a pipe or hose. Some valves are like faucets. They start or stop the flow of liquid or gas when you turn them with your hand. A special kind of valve in a scuba outfit automatically lets the diver get more air when he goes down deep. Another special valve lets the diver breathe used air out into the water. It also doesn't let any water come in when the diver breathes in.

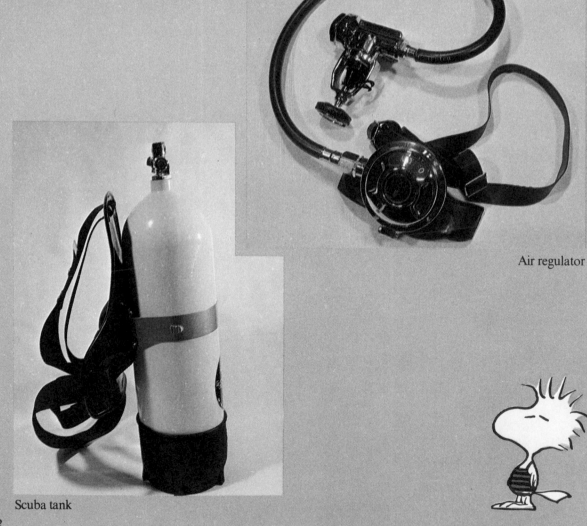

Air regulator

Scuba tank

Who invented modern scuba equipment?

Jacques Cousteau (ZHOCK koo-STOE), the famous ocean scientist who makes nature films for television. But he didn't do it all by himself. He had a partner named Emile Gagnan (ay-MEAL gah-NYOH). The two men were a perfect team. Cousteau was an ocean diver in the French navy. Gagnan was an engineer who knew a lot about all kinds of valves.

Cousteau knew that old-fashioned diving equipment was unsafe. Divers sometimes couldn't get enough air when they went down very deep. He figured that a new kind of valve was needed to control the amount of air coming out of the diver's tank. Gagnan was able to make the kind of valve Cousteau wanted. Cousteau and Gagnan completed their invention in 1943.

Jacques Cousteau (center)

What does "scuba" mean?

"Scuba" is a word made from the initials of the words "*s*elf-*c*ontained *u*nderwater *b*reathing *a*pparatus." Words made from the initials of other words are called acronyms (ACK-ruh-nimz). Acronyms help people save time in talking and writing by changing a bunch of big words into one little word.

How did the vacuum cleaner get its name?

When a vacuum cleaner is turned on, a fan keeps blowing out most of the air from its tank. A space with no air inside it is called a vacuum. A space with only a little bit of air inside it is called a partial (PAR-shul) vacuum. As the air goes out of a vacuum cleaner's tank, a partial vacuum is left. That is why the machine is called a "vacuum" cleaner.

How does a vacuum cleaner pick up dirt?

By using suction. The vacuum cleaner's fan blows air out of its tank or bag and leaves a partial vacuum inside. If you make an opening in the side of the container of a vacuum or a partial vacuum, air will rush in to fill the empty space. This is called suction.

Along with the air that rushes into a vacuum cleaner come dust and dirt. The air is blown out again. But the dust and dirt are caught in the dust bag, which is made of filter paper or finely woven cloth. When the bag is full, you can throw it away or empty it and use it again.

How can a weather forecaster tell when it is going to rain?

Weather depends on what the air is like. Weather forecasters know that clear, dry air is heavier than wet, stormy air.

Forecasters use a machine called a barometer (buh-ROM-ih-tur) to measure just how heavy the air is in any one area. There are many weather stations all over the country. In each one is a barometer. A forecaster looks at the barometer a few times each day. He or she checks to see whether the air is getting lighter or heavier. If the air is getting lighter in a certain place, that's a sign that rain is coming. If the air in a rainy place starts getting heavier, that's a sign that clear weather is coming.

661

How does a barometer tell how heavy the air is?

A barometer works by measuring how hard the air pushes something movable. One very popular type of barometer uses a heavy silvery liquid called mercury as the movable thing. The mercury moves up and down inside a long glass tube. Nothing else is inside this tube, not even air. The tube is sealed at the top and open at the bottom. The bottom is set in a little cup filled with mercury.

A mercury barometer works like a soda straw. When you suck on the straw, you take air out of it. But the air all around the soda presses on it. This air pressure forces the soda up inside the empty straw and into your mouth. The mercury inside the barometer tube is held up by the pressure of the outside air on the mercury in the cup. Heavy air pushes harder than light air and makes the mercury go farther up the tube. There is a yardstick alongside the tube so a person can see exactly how high the mercury stands.

Clear, heavy air will push the mercury a little more than 30 inches (76 centimeters) up the tube. Light, stormy air will push the mercury about 29 inches (about 74 centimeters) up the tube. That's not much of a difference. But it's enough to help the weather forecaster decide whether a day will be sunny or stormy.

NO, MEN. BREAKING THE GLASS IN THE BAROMETER WILL NOT STOP THE STORM...

662

Do all barometers have liquid in them?

No. There is a very popular type called the aneroid (AN-uh-royd) barometer. "Aneroid" means no liquid. Many people have this type of barometer in their homes, hanging on a wall or sitting on a shelf. An aneroid barometer looks something like a clock, but it has only one hand. Its numbers show how high the mercury would be if you had a mercury barometer.

The main part of an aneroid barometer is a hollow box or can. Inside is a vacuum. The sides of the box or can are made of springy metal. Air from outside the box always presses on the sides of the box. When the air presses, the sides move in. Clear, heavy air presses them in farther than stormy, light air. Levers connect the box to the hand on the front of the barometer. In this way, the hand points to a high number when the air pressure is high. It points to a low number when the air pressure is low.

Who invented the barometer?

Evangelista Torricelli (tore-ih-CHELL-lee) invented the barometer in 1643. But the first *weather-forecasting* barometer was made by Otto von Guericke (GAY-rih-keh) in the 1670s. It was about 34 feet (more than 10 meters) tall and used water instead of mercury. A water barometer needs to be much taller than a mercury barometer. That is because water weighs much less than mercury. Since water is lighter, the weight of the air pushes water higher than it pushes mercury.

Otto von Guericke

A scientist named Blaise Pascal (BLEZ pas-KALL) once made a barometer filled with red wine. He used red wine instead of water because it was easier to see inside a glass tube. Since wine weighs less than water, Pascal needed a tube 46 feet (14 meters) tall.

What makes a spray can squirt?

Inside a spray can is compressed gas. Compressed gas is like the air in a blown-up balloon. If you let go of the opening of the balloon, the air will rush out. The compressed gas in a spray can would also rush out. But it can't do this until you push the button on top of the can. Pressing the button is like opening a faucet. You are giving the compressed gas a place to go. As it rushes out, it pushes the liquid (paint, shaving cream, or insect killer) out before it. The liquid comes out as a fine spray. A spring makes the button pop up when you stop pressing it.

What makes a fire extinguisher squirt?

Fire extinguishers use compressed gas to make them squirt. The gas for most extinguishers is pumped in at the factory. But one type of extinguisher makes compressed gas when you turn it upside down. This type is called a soda-acid extinguisher.

The soda in soda-acid is not the kind you drink. It is a chemical called baking soda. The acid is a chemical called sulfuric (sull-FYOOR-ick) acid.

The extinguisher is filled with water. Soda is dissolved in the water. In the top of the extinguisher is a small bottle of sulfuric acid. When you turn the extinguisher upside down, the acid mixes with the water and baking soda. As a result, a lot of carbon dioxide gas is formed. It is under pressure inside the extinguisher. As soon as a compressed gas is given room, it will spread out. Because there is an opening in the extinguisher, the compressed carbon dioxide rushes out. The opening leads to a hose. The gas goes out through the hose and pushes the water out.

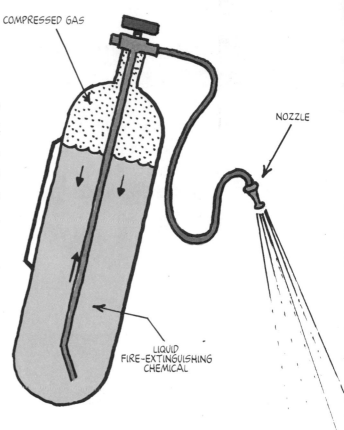

COMPRESSED GAS

NOZZLE

LIQUID FIRE-EXTINGUISHING CHEMICAL

GOOD GRIEF! IT'S ONLY PIG-PEN! I THOUGHT IT WAS A WALKING BRUSH FIRE!

665

How does a fire extinguisher put out fires?

Fires need two things to keep going: a gas called oxygen, and fuel. Fuel is anything that can get hot enough to burn. Some extinguishers cool the fuel. Others keep oxygen (which is in the air) away from the fuel.

Extinguishers that squirt water work mostly by cooling the fuel until it is too cold to burn. Extinguishers that squirt carbon dioxide make the fuel very cold—colder than ice. They also drive oxygen away from the fire. Some extinguishers squirt a dry chemical powder. It forms a crust on the fuel. The crust keeps oxygen away from the fuel. Another type of extinguisher coats the fuel with foam. The foam looks something like shaving cream. The foam keeps oxygen away from the fuel.

Did people have fire extinguishers 100 years ago?

Yes. People had them more than 150 years ago.

The fire extinguisher was invented by an Englishman named George Manby in 1813. His was a metal tank with water and compressed air in it. The compressed air made the water squirt out when a faucet was turned.

What machine is used to chop holes in pavement?

Have you ever heard of a jackhammer, an air hammer, or a pneumatic (new-MAT-ick) drill? Those are three names for the same machine. It is used to chop holes in sidewalks.

A jackhammer runs on compressed air. The air is pumped into the jackhammer through a hose. A trigger in the handle starts and stops the flow of air.

Inside the jackhammer is a hollow tube called a cylinder (SILL-in-dur). It looks something like a tin can. Inside the cylinder is a piece of metal called a piston. The piston can slide up and down inside the cylinder.

When the jackhammer is turned on air comes into the top of the cylinder. It pushes the piston down very hard. The piston then slams into a chisel that sticks out of the bottom of the jackhammer. The chisel is a metal bar. It is pointed on the end that touches the pavement. The hard blow of the piston drives the chisel into the pavement.

Next, air comes into the *bottom* of the cylinder and pushes the piston back up. When the piston reaches the top of the cylinder, the air changes direction again. The piston goes down and slams into the chisel again. The piston goes up and down more than 1,000 times a minute. It strikes the chisel very hard each time. Every time the piston hits the chisel, the chisel chops away a little piece of pavement.

667

How does a bicycle pump work?

A bicycle pump compresses air. One common kind is made up of a handle, a cylinder, a valve, a hose, and a metal disk with a gasket around it.

A gasket is a ring that fills an open space to make a pump or pipe leakproof. A gasket is sometimes made of rubber and sometimes of metal.

When you pull up on the handle of a bicycle pump, two things happen. First, the gasket hangs down loose and limp. This lets air go past it into the lower part of the cylinder. Second, the valve closes. So the air stays squeezed inside the bottom of the cylinder.

When you push down on the handle, the gasket presses tightly against the cylinder. It makes a tight seal. The air cannot get back up past the disk. But compressed air wants to spread out. Where can it go? When you push down on the handle, the valve opens. The air rushes out through the valve into the hose. From the hose the air goes into your bicycle tire.

I KNOW WHAT YOU MEAN...SOME DAYS ARE LIKE THAT!

What makes a popgun shoot?

Popguns work on compressed air. When you pull the trigger, a spring pushes a piston forward inside the barrel. All the air in the gun barrel is squeezed into a tiny space. This makes a lot of pressure build up. The pressure is so great that the cork at the end of the barrel can't hold the air in. The cork shoots out, and you hear a loud popping sound at the same time. The popping sound is really a small explosion. An explosion is what happens when a compressed gas suddenly bursts out of the place where it was held.

How does a car's brake pedal stop the car?

When a driver steps on a brake pedal, a chain of events begins. The pedal pushes a lever. The lever pushes a piston in a cylinder full of liquid. The piston pushes the liquid into four hoses. Each hose leads to one of the four wheels of the car. The liquid flows into a cylinder next to each wheel. There the liquid pushes more pistons. These pistons push curved pieces of metal against cylinders called brake drums. The brake drums are attached to the wheels. The rubbing of the metal slows down the turning of the wheels. So the car slows down and finally stops. When the driver stops pushing the brake pedal, springs pull the curved pieces of metal away from the brake drums. Then the wheels are free to turn again.

Do trains have the same kind of brakes as cars?

Not exactly. Trains need very powerful brakes—much more powerful than the pressure of one person pushing on a pedal with one foot. Train brakes use compressed air. The compressor is in the front of the train's locomotive. Hoses take the air to all the wheels. When the driver puts on the brakes, compressed air rushes into the hoses. The air pushes against some pistons. These pistons push curved pieces of metal against the wheels to slow down their turning.

Big trucks use the same kind of brakes as trains.

What makes a car-lifting machine go up and down?

You have probably seen the machine used in gasoline stations to lift a car into the air. It has a big, shiny metal tube that comes up out of the floor. That metal tube is really a giant piston. The piston fits into a pipe or cylinder buried in the floor. When the mechanic wants to lift the car, he turns on a pump. This pump forces liquid into the cylinder and pushes the piston up. When the car is raised high enough, the mechanic closes a kind of faucet called a valve. This keeps the liquid in the cylinder. The liquid keeps the piston from sliding back down into the floor. Then the mechanic turns off the pump. Now it is safe for him to go under the car and fix it. The car can't fall as long as liquid stays in the cylinder. When the mechanic wants to let the car down, he opens the valve. The liquid slowly leaves the cylinder and goes into a storage tank. As the liquid leaves the cylinder, the piston slowly sinks into the floor.

Weather forecasters use a tool called an anemometer (ann-uh-MOM-ih-turr) to measure the speed of the wind. Usually it has four arms with cups on them. When the wind blows against the cups, they move the arms, which makes a shaft spin around. The shaft turns a mechanism that moves a pointer on a dial. The pointer shows just how fast the wind is blowing. An anemometer works very much like a car's speedometer.

Anemometer

I SHOWED MY ANEMOMETER DRAWING IN SCHOOL TODAY, AND EVERYONE LAUGHED

THAT'S TOO BAD... BUT DON'T LET THEM DISCOURAGE YOU....

I'M GLAD YOU SAID THAT... I FEEL THE SAME WAY... WHY SHOULD I LET THEM DISCOURAGE ME?

I THINK I'LL QUIT SCHOOL!

Automatic sprinkler systems help protect buildings from fires. If you look at the ceiling in a public building or a warehouse, you may see small metal knobs sticking down. These are sprinkler heads.

The sprinkler heads are connected to water pipes like the ones that go to your faucet. If the temperature in the room gets too hot, part of the sprinkler head melts. That lets the water in the pipes rain down from the ceiling to help put out the fire.

Inside the pipes, the flowing water triggers a special alarm. Ringing bells warn people to leave the building. And the alarm system sends a message to the nearest firehouse so that the fire fighters will come quickly.

Windmills are machines that make wind do work. The earliest windmills were used to pump water or to grind grain into flour. The wind moved a set of blades or sails, which made a shaft turn. The turning shaft could be used to operate a pump or make a heavy millstone roll around on a pile of grain, crushing it into flour. These early windmills were invented before people had engines and motors to help with work. In windy places, it was cheaper to use a windmill for grinding or pumping than to get horses or people to do the work. Wind is free, but you need money to pay people and buy food for horses.

The newest windmills in use today are used to generate electricity. A windmill's turning shaft can drive an electrical generator just as well as it can drive a pump or a millstone. And it can drive a generator more cheaply than an engine or turbine that runs on expensive oil.

A dishwashing machine doesn't scrub plates to get them clean or wipe them to get them dry. Instead, powerful sprayers whirl around inside the machine. They send out jets of hot, soapy water to clean the plates. The soapy water is pumped out. Then the sprayers shoot clean hot water at the plates to rinse them. Finally, an electric heater warms up the air inside the dishwasher. The hot air helps the dishes to dry.

I'M TALLER THAN YOU, SO GO OUT IN THE KITCHEN AND STACK THE DISHWASHER!

GIVE ME ONE GOOD REASON WHY BEING TALLER MEANS YOU CAN TELL ME WHAT TO DO!

I CAN HIT FROM ABOVE!

I SHOULD HAVE ASKED FOR SOME MORE REASONS